CRYPTOCURRENCY FOR BEGINNERS

A Complete Guide To Becoming The Next Millionaire This Year And Beyond Investing In Cryptocurrencies. Beginner's Friendly.

Richie Gold

Copyright©2021. Richie Gold

All Right Reserved

INTRODUCTION

CHAPTER ONE

The most effective method to become a crypto master
What Capabilities Should you have to be a Cryptocurrency Master?
As a Novice, Where Would it be advisable for me to Begin in Crypto money?
Range Of Abilities Needed For A Digital Currency Master
Sixteen (16) Digital Currencies To Put Resources Into In 2021 That Are Both Modest And Productive

CHAPTER TWO

Top Digital Currencies Set To Soar Higher:
What are the best digital currencies?
Top Best Crypto Money Trades
What are the best crypto forms of money?
Best Crypto Money Trades Explained

CHAPTER THREE

Benefits of crypto forms of money
Disadvantage of digital currencies
Components To Search For In Good Digital Currency
What's better, Bitcoin or altcoins?
What is an Altcoin?
Attempt Coinbase

CHAPTER FOUR

Digital Money Guideline

CRYPTO ETF ENDORSEMENT
MORE EXTENSIVE INSTITUTIONAL DIGITAL CURRENCY RECEPTION
HOW MORE INSTITUTIONAL RECEPTION AFFECTS FINANCIAL BACKERS
BITCOIN'S FUTURE VIEWPOINT
OTHERS ARE MORE BULLISH ON BITCOIN'S MOMENTARY DEVELOPMENT.
HOW BITCOIN VALUE UNPREDICTABILITY AFFECTS FINANCIAL BACKERS

CHAPTER FIVE

CONCLUSION

INTRODUCTION

Cryptocurrency is a digital money or digital currency that isn't managed by a central structure like an organization or government. Taking everything into account, it relies upon blockchain advancement, with Bitcoin being the most notable one. As digital cash continues to procure traction on Cash Street, an always expanding number of decisions become available. There are at this point more than 6,000 digital types of cash accessible in the market.

While you can utilize crypto money to make buys, the vast majority treat it as drawn-out speculation. Be that as it may, unpredictability makes putting resources into digital money hazardous, so realize what you're getting into before you purchase in.

We've seen Bitcoin hit another unequaled excessive cost in April and October 2021, administrative discussions with the potential to hugely affect the business and more institutional purchases from significant organizations. Meanwhile, individuals' premium in crypto has soared this year: it's an intriguing issue among financial shareholders as well as in mainstream society as well, on account of everybody from long-standing financial backers like Elon Musk to that child from your secondary school on Twitter.

In numerous ways, 2021 has been a forward leap, says expert and head of Global Development at Gemini, a well-known digital money exchange. There's gigantic concentration and consideration being paid to the crypto industry.

CHAPTER ONE

The most effective method to become a crypto master

In the event that you love technology and have a premium in web-based investment, a vocation as a crypto money master could see you partaking in a long period of fascinating position jobs and extraordinary monetary prizes. Digital cash has seen a colossal expansion as of late, with work postings for crypto money and digital cash specialists ascending by a tremendous 194% from 2017-2018 as indicated by Beast. There is the potential for colossal development inside this industry, with digital cash being a fundamental piece of numerous organizations.

What Capabilities Should you have to be a Cryptocurrency Master?

In case you're not currently acquainted with the intricate details of the crypto money world, then, at that point, enlisting on an internet-based Blockchain course, for example, the Prologue to Blockchain and Crypto money course here at Courses Online can assist you with kicking start your profession in the crypto cash world. Enlist on this internet-based course and you can fit finding out with regards to crypto cash around your present work and life responsibilities; acquiring a top to bottom information on this captivating world from the nuts and bolts to the intricacies of the Digital speculation world.

As a Novice, Where Would it be advisable for me to Begin in Crypto money?

Just as being tech-disapproved and knowing about blockchain innovation, a Crypto money Master should have the option to stay aware of the most recent improvements in the advanced speculation world, just as know about Java, Python, Ethereum, and other web-based stages. You'll likewise have to ensure you have the right range of abilities (see beneath) and that you're being proactive with regards to your learning of the relative multitude of ideas that element in this field.

Range Of Abilities Needed For A Digital Currency Master

- Information on and energy for blockchain innovation
- Information on different programming language like Java and Python
- Certified to the obligation to deep-rooted learning
- Paying attention to details
- Tolerance

- Information on bitcoin conventions

Sixteen (16) Digital Currencies To Put Resources Into In 2021 That Are Both Modest And Productive

The digital currency market incorporates many diverse crypto forms of money, including Bitcoin, Ethereum, Tie, and Dogecoin. Putting resources into crypto forms of money can be overwhelming in the event that you have never done it since such countless monetary standards exist. Likewise, the precarious cost of Bitcoins (around $60k) and Ethereums (around $4000) makes these very famous digital forms of money hard for amateurs to put resources into. One more benefit of putting resources into digital money is the withdrawal of club rewards to your crypto wallet.

While there are a lot of ways of putting resources into digital money, 7b crypto specialist application may be probably the most ideal choice for dealers who need an unknown and secure stage. Permitting exchanging of in excess of 400 digital currencies, including BTC, ETH, DOGE, etc, 7b dealer gives up to 2 BTC everyday withdrawals, with no KYC required.

Numerous organizations and organizations are utilizing crypto forms of money nowadays, however, the Android application improvement organization is one of the organizations that utilization digital currencies fiercely. On the off chance that you are confounded with regards to which digital currency to put resources into, read along. In this article, you will find out with regards to the main 15 crypto forms of money that are both modest and productive.

1. Bitcoin

Initially planned by mysterious maker Satoshi Nakamoto in 2009, Bitcoin (BTC) is the main digital money. The blockchain behind BTC, as most digital forms of money, records exchanges across a great many PCs utilizing a circulated record.

2. Litecoin

Bitcoin is identical to gold in a crypto money world, while Litecoin is comparable to silver. Litecoin is a confided-in elective coin, just as one that is among the first. The Litecoin market cap is $2.59B, which is steep, and the coin has a quicker exchange speed than Bitcoin.

3. Ethereum

The Ethereum stage offers non-fungible tokens (NFTs), which are carried out naturally utilizing predefined boundaries alongside keen agreements. It is a top pick among developers since it offers brilliant agreements and NFTs.

4. Dogecoin

A Dogecoin venture could deliver returns up to almost half by 2021 whenever estimated around Rs. 50. Musk, who dispatched Dogecoin in 2013, showed up on a Program in May and discussed it. Dogecoin's worth took off ten times after this discussion yet has since fallen by 40%. One of the most encouraging digital currencies for 2021 is Dogecoin, which has as of late filled in unmistakable quality. There is a record-breaking $80 billion market worth of Dogecoin.

5. VeChain

In case you're searching for a modest Digital coin to put resources into, VeChain may be a possibility for you. VeChain Thor is the blockchain that powers VeChain Thor, just as the VeChain money. The circulated record works with the administration of supply chains and other business processes with this sort of blockchain.

6. Binance Coin (BNB)

Binance Coin, a digital money, is one of the top crypto trades all around the world and can trade products and installments. With the dispatch of

Binance Coin in 2017, it has adjusted to work with something other than exchanges on Binance. With it, one can purchase, sell, and cycle installments, just as book travel. You can likewise trade the digital currency for other crypto forms of money like Bitcoin or Ethereum just as exchange.

7. XRP or Wave

One of the most famous crypto forms of money of 2017 was Wave, otherwise called XRP. It was picked by worldwide financial organizations as their favored cash– turning into a quietly utilized strategy for sending and getting installments.

8. Fundamental Consideration Token

In 2018 and into 2019, BAT's cost held consistent as an image of its future potential. With Fearless' quick reception starting around 2019, the Fundamental Consideration Token capacities as a utility token. As one of the world's most well-known crypto forms of money, BAT has these provisions.

9. Cardano (ADA)

Evidence of stake turned into the norm in the crypto world from the get-go for Cardano. Not at all like stages like Bitcoin, where exchange check is a cutthroat, critical thinking activity, this technique wipes out this part to accelerate exchange time and lessen energy utilization and outflows.

Decentralized applications and savvy contracts on Cardano can likewise be constructed utilizing ADA, the local digital currency.

10. Monero

Look at Monero in case you are worried about private exchanges. Digital currency Monero improves the protection of its clients by making it profoundly fluid. This current digital money's emphasis on protection and liquidity may appear to be outdated to nerds, however, it is a decent decision for broadened contributing in view of its attention on security and liquidity.

11. XLM

Heavenly Lumens (XLM) are the cash inside the open-source blockchain framework Heavenly. XLM is essentially committed to giving minimal expense exchanging stages to developing business sectors.

12. (SUSHI)

Sushi, otherwise called SushiSwap, began as a decentralized trade that matched Uniswap. Since its beginning, its designers have overhauled the application to have a set-up of elements, with more use-cases coming out soon. What makes Sushi unique in relation to Uniswap is that Sushi delivers profits to Sushi token holders. Proprietors of SUSHI can stake their tokens on the stage to get 0.05% exchanging charges from all exchanges on the stage.

13. Tether

The Tether is not quite the same as other digital forms of money, for example, bitcoin. Its worth is supported by fiat monetary forms like dollars and euros, which keeps the worth of one of these categories theoretically. Tether's worth is considered more reliable.

14. EOS

As of now, it has been demonstrated to be a valuable blockchain. Numerous Android application improvement administrations utilize this digital money. Aside from wiping out exchange expenses, one of EOS's features is its interesting blockchain structure. A more noteworthy number of exchanges happen with this framework than with enormous installment networks like Visa and MasterCard.

15. Polygon

The blockchains of Polygon are interconnected, and Ethereum firmware is utilized to control this organization. Ethereum's concerns are overwhelmed by utilizing a sidechain produced using creative innovation.

16. Beam

Similarly, as with Monero, Shaft additionally utilizes a new blockchain called Mimblewimble, yet in contrast to Monero, it is security-centered. Utilizing this innovation, exchanges are quick while staying private. 4.99B USD is the market cap.

In case you are one of those individuals who are new to the digital money world, then, at that point, these 16 digital currencies are the most ideal decisions for you. These 16 will show expected development and are likewise modest. In any case remember that digital forms of money are exceptionally unpredictable, and nobody can foresee the conduct of the market. In this way, pick your crypto forms of money admirably and use them.

With a huge number of digital currencies available, it tends to be difficult to translate between a promising task with long haul development potential and speedy money gets that will not endure through a bear market. Thinking about a digital money's market capitalization, improvement group, market position, and future value potential, we've assembled a rundown of probably the best digital currencies to put resources into for 2021 and then some.

Regularly, altcoins are higher danger ventures when contrasted with Bitcoin, however, they frequently give better yields in a buyer market. On the other hand, altcoins commonly deteriorate more in bear markets. As a general rule, crypto forms of money with more modest market capitalization are more unpredictable than enormous, more settled digital currencies like Bitcoin and Ethereum. The coins on this rundown are inside the main 100 biggest crypto forms of money, and each task has a market capitalization in excess of $1 billion.

Investigate our rundown of the best digital currencies for 2021 and begin putting resources into the fate of money today.

CHAPTER TWO
Top Digital Currencies Set To Soar Higher:

- The best store of significant worth digital money: Bitcoin (BTC)
- Holds the most market excitement: Ethereum (ETH)
- Most encouraging layer 2 token: Polygon (MATIC)
- Best decentralized application: (SUSHI)
- Best fence against ETH: Cardano (ADA)
- Most noteworthy development potential: Chainlink (LINK)

What are the best digital currencies?
1. **Bitcoin (BTC)**

2. **Ethereum (ETH)**

3. **Polygon (MATIC)**

4. **(SUSHI)**

5. **Cardano (ADA)**

6. **Chainlink (LINK)**

Top Best Crypto Money Trades

What are the best crypto forms of money?

The best crypto forms of money in 2021 are not simply monetary standards, they're local resources for the absolute most encouraging new businesses and ventures in the monetary world. Imprint Cuban and Andreessen Horowitz both vigorously put resources into altcoins, explicitly decentralized money (Defi) speculations that have been famous crypto ventures this year. Here are probably the most encouraging VC-moved digital forms of money to purchase in 2021.

1. Bitcoin (BTC)

The ruler of all digital forms of money, Bitcoin, was the first and the most notable crypto money available. It likewise profits by the biggest market cap and is among the most profoundly exchanged crypto forms of money, guaranteeing liquidity to financial shareholders. Bitcoin is the ruler with regards to retail and institutional reception. Most altcoins will pursue Bitcoin's value direction, so if Bitcoin does ineffectively, it's probable altcoins will drain as well.

Considering the cost of bitcoin is still down from everything time highs of more than $64,000, purchasing presently might be a wise interest into what's to come. There will just at any point be 21 million bitcoin in the presence (with around 15% of this number being lost), so as long as Bitcoin's client base keeps on developing, so will the cost of the resource. Bitcoin right now has an expansion pace of 1.7%, and this rate parts at regular intervals in what's known as the bitcoin halving.

2. Ethereum (ETH)

As the money and stage that made shrewd agreements some portion of the digital currency market's jargon, Ethereum has seen gigantic increases since its presentation in 2015. As of now just behind Bitcoin concerning market capitalization, Ethereum has become one of the most broadly examined crypto money projects on the planet.

A consortium of the absolute greatest names in the business, including Microsoft, Intel, Pursue, and J.P. Morgan are building business-prepared adaptations of the product that drives Ethereum. With the force and market excitement behind the Ethereum project, there's not any justification to think Ethereum has run its course, and financial backers ought to think about Ethereum as a component of their crypto money portfolio. Ethereum is accessible on Coinbase, Gemini and Blockchain.

3. Polygon (MATIC)

Polygon is an Ethereum sidechain that is scaling DeFi at a fast rate. Ethereum's high gas expenses have featured the organization's battle to move up to Eth2. Ethereum prime supporter, Vitalik Buterin, has communicated his help for Layer 2 scaling arrangements, which handle exchanges on a side chain prior to presenting a clump of exchanges to Ethereum's layer 1 blockchain. Thus, clients pay fundamentally fewer exchange charges and can settle exchanges in only a couple of moments.

Layer 2 sidechains assume a basic part in scaling Ethereum, and Polygon is one of the first to do it. Resources should be spanned to the sidechain, so there are some exchanging costs that will prompt individuals to remain on Polygon as long as possible. Polygon is accessible on Coinbase and Gemini.

4. (SUSHI)

Sushi, otherwise called SushiSwap, began as a decentralized trade that equaled Uniswap. Since its origin, its engineers have updated the application to have a set-up of provisions, with more use-cases coming out soon. What makes Sushi unique in relation to Uniswap is that Sushi delivers profits to Sushi token holders. Proprietors of SUSHI can stake their tokens on the stage to get 0.05% exchanging expenses from all exchanges on the stage.

Besides the SushiSwap DEX, the decentralized application has loaning markets, token launchpads, and even influence exchanging. Sushi intends to dispatch Shoyu, and NFT stage that will rival OpenSea, the biggest NFT commercial center today. A 2.5% expense will be charged to NFT merchants, which will be paid out to SUSHI token holders as profits.

5. Cardano (ADA)

Cardano is perhaps Ethereum's biggest rival. The venture was established by Charles Hoskinson, one of Ethereum's past prime supporters. The crypto money is now evidence of stake, an agreement calculation that Ethereum is as yet during the time spent relocating over to. Evidence of-Stake doesn't just take into account quicker and less expensive exchanges; however, it is likewise harmless to the ecosystem.

Ethereum beats Cardano on its DeFi (decentralized money) environment. Cardano still can't seem to deliver keen agreements on its foundation, however, the crypto money intends to add this component in 2021. Ethereum as of now has many decentralized applications on its foundation, and the organization has a lot a greater number of clients than Cardano's. Cardano is accessible on Coinbase and Gemini.

6. Chainlink (LINK)

Chainlink (LINK) is an Ethereum token that controls the Chainlink decentralized prophet organization. This organization permits savvy contracts on Ethereum to safely associate with outside information sources, APIs, and installment frameworks.

Chainlink entered the market in 2014 under the name SmartContract.com. Soon after its dispatch, the name changed to Chainlink to more readily address its center market.

Chainlink set up an essential organization with Google in 2019. The arrangement got Chainlink's convention inside the Google brilliant agreement methodology. This move was viewed as a significant success by financial shareholders as it permits clients to associate with Google's 2 most well-known cloud administrations. Chainlink is accessible on Coinbase and Gemini.

Best Crypto Money Trades Explained

The best crypto money trade for you relies upon your necessities as a financial investor. Whether or not you're a drawn-out holder or an informal investor, a trade's security ought to be among your first concerns. U.S-based trades give high security, normally offering 2-factor confirmation and cold stockpiling for your crypto resources.

Among the crypto money trades available, Coinbase, Gemini, and Binance are probably the best places to begin putting resources into crypto. Gemini is extraordinary in light of the fact that it helps you acquire revenue on your digital currency positions only for holding the resource; in case you're a long-term holder, this is an incredible methodology to aggregate more coins. Coinbase has the best UI (User Interface) of the 3 options, and its Coinbase Learn Program pays financial shareholders in crypto for finding out about blockchain innovation!

The first digital currency was Bitcoin, created in 2009 by a mysterious designer named Satoshi Nakamoto. The market doesn't have the foggiest idea about the genuine character of Satoshi Nakamoto, yet the foundation laid by the development of Bitcoin made it ready for other Digital monetary forms.

It likewise prompted the developing acknowledgment of digital currencies as both a speculation opportunity and as a mode of trade, an approach to safely move cash starting with one money proprietor then onto the next carefully and without the utilization of customary banks or monetary foundations.

Crypto forms of money are intended to work as cash, an option in contrast to the fiat monetary standards of the world, a significant number of which are in different phases of disintegration through swelling or are in danger of government seizure. Greece, a country with a 45% personal expense rate, seizes more than 900 financial balances each day.

The island country of Cyprus, a growing monetary focus, endured the fallouts of Greek obligation defaults, driving Cyprus' administration to hold onto contributor's assets to stay dissolvable. Venezuela's swelling rate is right now more than 46,000%, which makes a monetary emergency that undermines the endurance of families in the country. Crypto forms of money offer a fence against swelling, particularly in nations like Venezuela.

CHAPTER THREE

Benefits of crypto forms of money

Crypto forms of money offer a few benefits when contrasted and customary banking, cash moves, and fiat monetary standards.

Security.

Numerous crypto forms of money are planned in light of protection and dark the character of the sender and beneficiary of digital currency reserves. Just money gives comparable namelessness. Note that some digital money, as Bitcoin and Ethereum, are just pseudo-mysterious. When one can append a digital currency address to your character, they're ready to see every one of the exchanges you've made with that crypto address.

Decentralization.

Digital money proprietors utilize a wallet to get to their cash and get or send assets from a particular wallet address that utilizes a mysterious key for access. Some likewise utilize a trade to store cash, albeit the training brings extra danger. The record of the money exists on the blockchain with a duplicate put away on each full hub, a PC that keeps a record locally and synchronizes with different PCs on the web. Your money isn't in a singular bank, or even a couple. The decentralized idea of crypto money records makes digital currencies less defenseless against seizure or restricted dangers, similar to flames or equipment disappointments. The information isn't simply put away off-site, it's replicated worldwide to every full hub.

Keen agreements (Smart Contract).

Some crypto forms of money have a remarkable element that can't be copied with fiat monetary standards. Ethereum is among the best models with its hearty help for brilliant agreements" basically programs that live on the blockchain and can be utilized to oversee exchanges just as various uses, some of which we probably won't have yet imagined. At a base level, these agreements can be utilized to supplant referees or escrow and other monetary administrations. Since brilliant agreements live on the blockchain, they're a permanent and secure way of taking care of cash.

Shortage.

Bitcoin has a decent stockpile. More than 17 million Bitcoin are in presence. Nonetheless, just 21 million Bitcoin will at any point exist. It's incorporated into the code for the money. The proper inventory gives Bitcoin and other digital currencies comparable attributes to gold, silver, or other valuable metals that have generally been utilized as cash. In contrast to U.S. Dollars, English Pounds or some other fiat cash, after the full stock is available for use, the stockpile won't ever develop, cheapening the money's purchasing influence.

Cost of moves.

The expense related with crypto money moves can be a master or a con, contingent upon the kind of cash, the sort of move, and the speed of the exchange. Bitcoin, for instance, can become costly on the off chance that you really wanted quick leeway for an exchange. Now and again, costs are less tricky for less time-touchy exchanges. Different kinds of digital forms of money, like Litecoin, are quick and cheap to move, prompting expanded reception of Wave based exchanges and related innovation by monetary foundations.

Disadvantage of digital currencies

Crypto forms of money accompany a rundown of contemplations that can assist financial investors with making more secure speculations. Since the blockchain business is as yet in its early stages, most digital currencies are profoundly unpredictable. This being said, some crypto forms of money, as stable coins, offer correct speculations with more significant yields than less secure ventures like land.

Market reception.

Mindfulness for Crypto forms of money is developing, however the majority of the attention has been on Bitcoin. Generally, couple of retailers acknowledge digital currencies for installment, yet there are a couple. Overstock.com declared in 2017 that they would acknowledge digital forms of money as installment. Installments will be restricted to Bitcoin, Ethereum, Litecoin, Dash, and Monero, treating the other 1,500+ digital forms of money with utter disdain.

Outdated nature.

Upwards of 1,000 crypto forms of money have flopped as of now, with additional to unquestionably follow. When in doubt of thumb, the more modest a coin's market cap is, the almost certain it is to fall flat. A few interesting points while checking whether an undertaking will be effective is its client base, specialized turns of events, and regardless of whether the task includes rivalry inside the digital currency space.

Deserted digital money projects.

A large portion of the venture cash for digital forms of money is centered around a somewhat little gathering of coins. Without financial backer premium, tasks can get deserted, leaving financial investors with basically useless crypto coins.

Guideline hazard.

In accordance with crypto forms of money, guideline hazard has different sides. In the U.S., crypto forms of money are not directed at a government level, passing on states the choice to present guidelines and guidelines with respect to digital currencies or the blockchain innovation that fills in as the spine for digital currencies. Then again, a few financial investors and money specialists have communicated worry over future guideline for digital currencies, which could cause a drop sought after or dispose of interest inside and out.

Liquidity hazard.

Financial investors and lesser-realized digital currencies might discover less purchasers, making difficulties when hoping to leave a position.

Instability hazard.

Scarcely any speculation classes can match crypto forms of money with regards to value unpredictability. Costs can rise or fall significantly in a solitary day, manifesting the moment of truth fortunes.

outsider danger. Mt. Gox, a Bitcoin trade situated in Japan, and the main trade worldwide in 2014 was hacked, prompting a deficiency of almost a large portion of a billion dollars in Bitcoin. Altogether, an expected 850,000 Bitcoins having a place with financial investors disappeared, eventually compelling the trade into chapter 11.

Secure keys.

Crypto forms of money are regularly kept in an Digital wallet, which is gotten by a long code or a long series of words. Not at all like your ledger or venture account, there is no recuperation interaction accessible in the event that you lose your secret word. Without your secret phrase, your digital money wallet and its substance are at this point not available.

Components To Search For In Good Digital Currency

Reception rate.

Digital forms of money are exceptionally speculative interests in the greatest increases are in some cases found among recently presented coins or coins whose innovation has discovered the market, similar to the case with Dogecoin. More wary financial backers might decide to see reception rate, zeroing in portfolio venture on digital forms of money that are right now utilized in true exchanges.

Market cap.

In numerous ways, the market cap for a given crypto money goes inseparably with liquidity. Youngster digital currencies may not at any point discover the market, keeping financial backers from leaving the position beneficially.

Promising new innovation.

Ethereum and Polygon both owe their stratospheric gains in 2017 to the inventive innovation incorporated into their particular stages, separating both digital currencies from the packed market of regularly comparable contributions.

Security or obscurity highlights.

Innovation like keen agreements, found in Ethereum and a few other digital currencies make exchanges safer by empowering a bunch of rules for every exchange. Some digital currencies like Monero place a solid spotlight on namelessness, clouding the character of the sender and recipient of assets.

Industry utility.

Ethereum and Polygon are again genuine instances of digital forms of money with utility past a basic mode of trade. Ethereum is the base layer of the decentralized money upheaval, and Polygon is the layer 2 where exchanges and savvy agreements can be executed at scale.

What's better, Bitcoin or altcoins?
Most crypto money financial investors decide to hold both Bitcoin and altcoins. Bitcoin is the most settled digital money, and it's more protected than most altcoin speculations. Nonetheless, altcoins frequently give better yields during a positively trending market, making them appealing speculations for hazard open minded people.

What is an Altcoin?
The term altcoin alludes to any crypto money other than Bitcoin. This being said, most financial investors don't allude to Ethereum as an altcoin, as it's huge environment and set up network put it in its very own classification.

Attempt Coinbase
Coinbase fabricates crypto items to help you purchase, sell, and store your bitcoin and digital money. You can purchase Bitcoin, Ethereum, Cardano, Solana, Chainlink, Uniswap and other DeFi tokens immediately. Temporarily, get a $10 BTC reward when you make your first exchange of $10 or more!

Rating the Top Digital currency Decisions
Run a speedy web-based quest and you'll discover many suggestions for how to put resources into digital currency. In picking the main sixteen picks, the accompanying variables were thought of.

Life span

How long has the digital money been near? New digital currencies aren't promptly precluded, however having chronicled information for correlation assists you with perceiving how an organization has performed up to this point.

History

How has the organization performed during its years in business? In the event that you see security in costs, that is a decent sign. In the event that you notice that the digital currency is acquiring footing and turning out to be more significant with time, that is surprisingly better.

Great To Know

Past execution isn't demonstrative of future execution. Whenever things can change, and a venture might perform preferable or more regrettable over it has previously.

Innovation

How does the stage contrast with others as far as ease of use and security? The principal thing you need to search for is the speed at which exchanges happen. The organization ought to have the option to deal with exchange traffic effortlessly.

You additionally need to ensure your speculation is secure. Most digital currencies use blockchain innovation, making all exchanges straightforward and simple to follow. Blockchain innovation doesn't really make it harder for programmers to take your crypto money. It makes it simpler to follow your speculation so it very well may be recuperated as opposed to being lost after extortion.

Reception Rate

What number of individuals are putting resources into the digital money you're thinking about? At the point when you see a significant degree of reception, that implies the digital money has better liquidity. Exchanging, selling or spending will be simpler later on.

CHAPTER FOUR

Digital Money Guideline

Anticipate proceeded with discussions about digital money guideline. Officials in Washington D.C. also, across the world are attempting to sort out some way to set up laws and rules to make digital money more secure for financial backers and less interesting to cybercriminals.

China declared in September that all digital currency exchanges in the nation are unlawful, viably slowing down any crypto-related exercises inside Chinese lines. In the U.S., things are less clear. Central bank Seat Jerome Powell said as of late that he has "no aim" of restricting digital currency in the U.S while Security and Trade Commission Executive Gary Gensler has reliably remarked on the two his own organizations and the Product Prospects Exchanging Commission's job in policing the business.

He likewise said financial investors are probably going to get injured if stricter guideline isn't presented. In addition, the IRS has an undeniable premium in ensuring financial backers realize how to report virtual cash when they record their expenses.

Like most things with digital currency, guideline accompanies obstacles. There are various organizations that might possibly have locale to supervise everything as said by specialists. What's more, it contrasts state by state."

Clear guideline would mean the expulsion of a critical road obstruction for digital currency since U.S. firms and financial investors are working without clear rules right now.

Administrative declarations can likewise influence the cost of digital currency in currently unpredictable business sectors. Market unpredictability is the reason contributing specialists prescribe keeping any digital currency speculations to under 5% of your all out portfolio contribute nothing you're not good with losing.

At last, numerous specialists accept guideline is something beneficial for the business. Reasonable guideline is a success for everybody. It gives individuals more trust in crypto, however it's something we need to take as much time as necessary on and we need to hit the nail on the head, as said by specialists.

Crypto ETF Endorsement
There's as of now been a significant forward leap on this front, with the principal Bitcoin ETF as of late making its presentation on the New York Stock

Trade. The improvement addresses a new and more regular way of putting resources into crypto. The BITO Bitcoin ETF permits financial backers to purchase in on digital money straightforwardly from customary venture businesses they may as of now have accounts with, similar to Constancy or Vanguard.

However, some say the BITO ETF isn't sufficient, in light of the fact that while the asset is connected to Bitcoin, it doesn't really hold the crypto straightforwardly. The asset rather holds Bitcoin prospects contracts. While Bitcoin fates pursue the overall directions of the real crypto, specialists say it may not follow the cost of Bitcoin straightforwardly. Until further notice, financial investors should keep sitting tight for an ETF that holds Bitcoin straightforwardly.

ETF endorsement has been in thought by the SEC on different occasions in the course of recent years, however BITO is quick to acquire endorsement.

How a crypto ETF affects financial backers

It's too early to tell the number of financial investors will get in on BITO — however the asset saw bunches of exchanging activity its first week. As a general rule, the more open digital money resources are inside customary speculation items, the more Americans could purchase in and impact the crypto market. Rather than figuring out how to explore a crypto money trade to exchange your Digital resources, you can add crypto to your portfolio straightforwardly from a similar financier with which you at this point have a retirement or other traditional endeavor account.

Be that as it may, putting resources into a crypto ETF, as BITO, actually conveys a similar danger as any crypto venture. It's as yet a speculative and unstable venture. In case you're not able to lose the cash you put into crypto by buying on a trade, then, at that point, you shouldn't place it in a crypto reserve by the same token. Cautiously consider in case you're willing to assume the danger of having digital money in your portfolio by any means.

More Extensive Institutional Digital Currency Reception

Standard organizations across ventures have taken revenue — and at times themselves put resources into — crypto money and blockchain in 2021. AMC, for instance, as of late reported it will actually want to acknowledge Bitcoin installments before the current year's over. Fintech organizations like PayPal and Square are additionally wagering on crypto by permitting clients to purchase on their foundation. Tesla keeps on going to and fro on its acknowledgment of Bitcoin installments, however the organization holds billions in crypto resources.

Specialists anticipate increasingly more of this up front investment.

A huge measure of inflow of consideration, and that will keep on driving the development of the business for some time presently, said a specialist.

A few specialists anticipate greater, worldwide organizations could kick off this reception much more in the last 50% of this current year. What we're taking a gander at is foundations engaging in crypto, regardless of whether it's Amazon or the enormous banks, says master. A tremendous retailer like Amazon could make a chain response of others tolerating it, and would add a ton of believability, as said master.

For sure, Amazon has as of late started bits of gossip that it's taking actions to that end by sharing a task posting for a "Digital money and blockchain item lead." Walmart is additionally enlisting a crypto master to administer its blockchain system.

How More Institutional Reception Affects Financial Backers

While paying for things in crypto forms of money doesn't bode well for a great many people at this moment, more retailers tolerating installments may change that scene later on. It'll probably be significantly longer before it'll be a shrewd monetary choice to spend Bitcoin on labor and products, yet further institutional reception could achieve more use-cases for regular clients, and thusly, affect crypto costs. Nothing is ensured, however on the off chance that you purchase crypto money as a drawn out store of significant worth, the more "genuine world" utilizes it has, the more probable interest and worth will increment.

Bitcoin's Future Viewpoint

Bitcoin is a decent pointer of the crypto market as a general rule, since it's the biggest crypto money by market cap and the remainder of the market will in general pursue its directions.

Bitcoin's cost has taken a wild ride so far in 2021, and in October set another unequaled excessive cost twice this year. This second record high of the year follows a past high mark of $60,000 in April and a resulting drop to under $30,000 as of late as July. This unpredictability is a major piece of why specialists prescribe keeping your crypto ventures to under 5% of your portfolio in any case.

However, how high will Bitcoin go? Bitcoin's past may give a few insights, as per Kiana Danial, creator of "Digital money Contributing for Fakers."

There have been a lot of enormous spikes followed by pullbacks in Bitcoin's cost starting around 2011. What is anticipated from Bitcoin is unpredictability present moment and long-haul development.

Others Are More Bullish On Bitcoin's Momentary Development.
The central specialized investigator at TokenMetrics, a digital currency stage, figures the cost of Bitcoin will move all through the remainder of the year. It is more probable Bitcoin goes to $75,000 than $25,000, He said.

How Bitcoin value unpredictability affects financial backers
Bitcoin's unpredictability is more justification for financial investors to play a consistent long game. In the event that you're purchasing for long haul development potential, don't stress over momentary swings. Everything thing you can manage isn't check out your digital money venture, or "set it and fail to remember it." As specialists keep on letting us know each time there's a value swing — regardless of whether up or down — passionate response can make financial backers act imprudently and settle on choices that outcome in misfortunes on their speculation.

CHAPTER FIVE

Conclusion

Digital currencies and decentralized monetary items are as yet in their early stages. In case you're new to digital currencies, you might be ideally serviced by contributing just danger capital and by building an arrangement of generally exchanged crypto forms of money. Beginning coin contributions can be enticing, especially with the explanatory ascents normal to ICOs. Nearly as normal is a steep fall following the ICO.

More settled monetary forms help to forestall a portion of the instability and furnish preferable liquidity over found with recently printed digital currencies. Realize where a crypto money can be exchanged and how huge the market is for that digital currency.

Numerous early financial backers have ended up without a feasible way of exiting the position. In case crypto forms of money are staying put, some generally excellent chances are probably going to exist among the most usually exchanged monetary standards, while likewise limiting danger because of deserted ventures or absence of liquidity.

In case you're completely hoping to contribute without executing inside the organization, recollect that digital money isn't a pyramid scheme. All things being equal, you ought to think of it as a drawn out speculation.

There's no doubt: Digital currencies are digging in for the long haul. The inquiry becomes, where is the best spot to put your cash on the lookout?

As you choose which digital currency is the best speculation for you, here are other things to remember:

The speed at which exchanges are finished

The expenses related with executing

The capacity to utilize your crypto money for normal buys and bank moves.

www.ingramcontent.com/pod-product-compliance
Lightning Source LLC
Chambersburg PA
CBHW050318220526
45465CB00005B/2036